BawB's Raven Feathers
Reflections on the simple things in life

VOLUME II

Robert Chomany

INVERMERE PRESS • CALGARY, CANADA

Copyright © 2013, Robert Chomany

All rights reserved. No part of this publication may be reproduced or transmitted in any form or by any means, electronic or mechanical, including photocopying, recording, or any information storage and retrieval system without permission in writing from the author.

ISBN 978-0-9918821-6-8 (v. 2 : softcover)

Illustration: Jessee Wise
Book Design: Fiona Raven Book Design
Chief Editor: Rachel Small, Faultless Finish Editing
Proofreader: Carrie Mumford

Published by
Robert Chomany
Calgary, Alberta, Canada
bchomany@telusplanet.net

Printed in the United States of America

www.bawbsravenfeathers.net

This series of books is dedicated to my mom—without her love, patience and guidance I would not be the man I am today. She taught me to appreciate compassion, to stand alone, and to be proud of who I am, and she gave me strength to pursue my dreams.

With your eyes you can see the beauty of living.

With your soul you can see the beauty of life.

Challenges

What does the word "challenge" mean to you? Back in the days of yore it meant picking up a lance and proving your worth as a knight. Today, it might mean getting to work on time. At some point over the years, the word "challenge" became common in our day-to-day conversations and lost its romance. No longer does a challenge begin with a glove slap to the face or the drop of a gauntlet. To me, a challenge is a glitch in an otherwise routine task.

The important thing to consider is whether you welcome challenges or fight them. The way you deal with challenges is often an indicator of how your life will unfold. For example, if you want a peanut butter sandwich but the cap on the jar of peanut butter seems welded on, how do you react? Do you get frustrated, put the jar on the shelf, and opt for plan B, a grilled cheese sandwich? Or do you go through every one of the tips and tricks you were taught to open a jar and wonder which one will work?

Whether we give up or try out different options when faced with a challenge is purely our own choice. We choose to react. We choose to accept failure and move on. We choose to strive for success and learn lessons along the way. I choose to believe failing means I tried, and after each attempt, I choose to learn new ways to deal with the challenge. Keep in mind that by welcoming the challenges life has to offer, you have an opportunity to learn, to better yourself, and to reward yourself after achieving success. By accepting whatever challenges come your way, you will learn to see the good or the lesson in all things.

Challenge can also involve getting out of your comfort zone. Every day is brand new. If you feel like you're in a rut, a pattern of conformity, challenge yourself to change it—just a bit, once a week, until you get stronger, until you start having fun being you again. Seek out new challenges, learn from failure; strive for success, reward yourself; take pride in yourself for trying, believe in yourself; and most importantly, believe that you can accomplish anything you put your mind to.

Any challenge you face is beatable, if you believe in who you are.

So you've hit the wall, frustration looms,
there's nothing you can do.
Take heart my friend, because in fact,
the answer lies in you.
A heart that's strong, a breath or two,
and patience to make things right,
are all you need to make it
through the worst of any plight.

Determination is your strength that comes from way down deep,
it's always there for you to use when your path becomes too steep.

Life is a mystery, sometimes it's a test,
share in your victories and learn from the rest.

Forgive yourself for your mistakes
and learn from others' too.
Grow with change and share your warmth
and troubles will be few.

There will be days when you can't see the light,
when your heart is dejected and you've run out of fight.
Listen then to your soul, it is there should you ask,
for an answer to solving your arduous task.

Look outside the box and most often you'll find,
a simple resolve can bring peace of mind.
Nothing in life can put out your glow,
if you smile and nod and then go with the flow.

It's never too late to learn from mistakes.

Start living by example, whatever it takes.

Sometimes in life you will come to a bridge
you really shouldn't cross,
you know what's there on the other side—
you're in for emotional loss.
Cheer up my friend, for your path is long,
you'll find another bridge,
one this time that leads to smiles
and sunlight on the ridge.

I've said it before and I'll say it once more—
tomorrow brings a new day,
and with it comes a fresh new look
at whatever comes your way.

See past the moments of yesterday,
and accept the request to leap.
Face the challenge that comes your way,
and smile when you're asked to dig deep.

You never know what you're capable of
until you're asked to do,
and whatever it is becomes more rewarding
if the one who is asking is you.

Take from life your failures
and the lessons that you've learned,
and give it back your knowledge
and the wisdom that you've earned.

Perception

Our lives are ruled by our own perceptions. We all perceive things differently, and I believe this is a major reason why we struggle to get along with one another at times. One person might perceive the simplest thing drastically differently than another person. Differences in perception can cause stress or tension, but they can also force us to open our minds to a more colorful version of life. For example, some may perceive a cloud to be just that—a mass of water vapor in the atmosphere—whereas others may perceive a cloud to be an image of a dog, a rocket ship, or a freshly baked chocolate cookie. How wonderful to have that perception.

There is no right or wrong way to perceive—your perception is yours alone. It can be tainted by another's opinion, but it will always remain yours. It helps you form opinions, either positive or negative, about things you have seen or heard. Perception is also based on context. For example, without auditory cues, your perception of something as basic as a text message could be entirely different than what the sender of the message intended you to perceive.

We are born with the gift of choice. In the worst of circumstances, we can choose to be happy with what we have. This is where perception is crucial. When you wake up every morning, how you perceive your life is what shapes your life for the rest of your life. If you perceive your life to be happy, then it will be. And just by choosing to wear a smile, you can change the perception others have of you. Opinions and impressions are formed almost immediately, and when you smile, others will perceive that you are a happy individual and are enjoying being you.

We all know how important it is to respect others' opinions, but it is also very important that we believe in ourselves and our own perception of things. You have every right to be yourself, to choose to believe things are the way they are because you see them that way, but you also have the choice to accept differences of opinion and perception to help create a smoother flow of energy in the world.

Perceive for yourself nothing but success in life.

Let your eyes be your guide to the world that surrounds,
then use your perception to create a world more profound.

Take ahold of life and look at things
from a different point of view.
When you control the way you roll,
life will work out for you.

It's tough sometimes to connect all the dots,
when those little dots are all that you've got.
Change your perspective and see the designs,
then all of those dots will become little lines.

You've heard this before, it should be no surprise:
you will find happiness, if you open your eyes.

Remember this, as you waste your day wishing,
something that is true:
a lot of people in the world right now
would love to be in your shoes.

The beauty of life surrounds us—
it's in everything new and old.
It's a gift that nature gives to us,
in all that we behold.
First calm your soul and free your mind,
and then perceive with your eyes.
The absolute beauty that is simply living
should come as no surprise.

Let go of your thoughts for a moment or two,
and you'll get a new grasp on what's real.
There's no need to focus on how things may seem,
but take notice of how you feel.

The clouds will always be up in the sky,
with nothing to portray.
How you choose to look at them
is what determines your day.

The world is a wonderful place for us all,
with lots of room for being.
We can always change our perception of things
if we don't like what we're seeing.

Today is a day just like yesterday,
but the difference today is you.
Instead of just thinking it's always the same,
try out something new.
Be the person with the big cheery smile,
the one who loves to live,
the one today who can simply enjoy,
all of what life has to give.

Doors don't always open right away;
sometimes you need a key,
determination and belief in you
works every time, you'll see.
You may just need a simple change
in the way you look at things;
focus on a dream you have,
feel the comfort it brings.

There are often clouds up in the sky—behind them the sun is shining;
the trick to staying positive is to look for silver linings.

Depending on your point of view, you have the upper hand:
fill your life with happiness or have it turn out bland.
Remind yourself to always find the positive in things,
and you will surely find elation in all your future brings.

Choice

We often take our ability to choose for granted. So often we just accept what life offers and live in an unbalanced state. Right at the start of our day, when the sun first kisses the horizon with its warm light, we can choose to be happy with everything we have and everything we are. We can choose to believe that life is a gift.

As our day progresses and we are faced with many other choices, again we can choose to be happy. The drive to work can be a time to gather thoughts and prepare for the day. We can choose to share a smile with others on the road. We don't need to amass a king's ransom or live in a palace to appreciate life—it is more important to recognize true wealth: friends, family, the pets we share a world with, and the ability to spread happiness with just a smile. This recognition is a choice.

When faced with challenges or issues, we have the choice to react or to resolve. Should we choose to resolve, we remain in a calmer state and can see past the issue at hand. Should we see others faced with difficulty we can choose to sit back and ignore them or offer to help. Sharing is also a choice and a gift, and we all have something to share—a story of adventure, a tip for an easier resolution, or our kindest gift of all: a hug or a smile.

Tomorrow comes, our lives go on. Time won't wait for us to make our choices, so choose to be happy. Live from your soul; choose to see the beauty of a butterfly's wings as well as its ability to fly. Find balance in your life, help others balance theirs, and appreciate living as a gift.

Life is full of choices, and I have chosen to live mine to the best of my ability. I'm learning each day to be happy with who I am, to be grateful for life and celebrate living, and to share my words, my light, and my smiles with the world. I have chosen to dance with the wind, to soar in bluest of skies on ebony wings, and to amble on a balanced path of soft earth.

I choose a way because I can, if I am given a choice.

How are you today? Did you wake with a smile?
Are you happy being you?
Did you roll out of bed with any wonderful thoughts,
excited the day is new?
This is it, you know, this life you're in,
it's your choice to make it real,
and it starts right now, with that very first thought
of how you choose to feel.

We all have a choice in shaping our day,
    so choose to put on a smile.
Decide to be happy right from the start,
    and you'll find it lasts a while.

You can't turn off the light in your soul—
it always shines in there,
the choice you have with each new day
is how much you want to share.

Live your life with no regrets, and believe in what you do,
make a choice and walk that path that right now is so new.

Sure you can wonder if you've made the right choice,
that's just being real,
but you alone are responsible,
for how things make you feel.
Choose to be happy with all that transpires,
and look forward to what will be.
Your future lies ahead of you,
beyond what you can see.

However you choose to live your life is entirely up you,
just remember the benefits of loving life in everything you do.
Make the time to rest a bit and learn to love just being,
appreciate the beauty that exists in everything you're seeing.

Find balance as every new day comes,
and learn each step you take.
Life is not always what you want,
but it's often what you make.

Have you ever been ambling, somewhat lost,
    like you have no direction to go?
Have you ever looked in a mirror to find
    you have no reflection to show?
It's time for a breath, a moment to gather
    your thoughts, and your balance too.
Take time to be still, revert to your will,
    and choose what is best for you.

They say life is short, but indeed it is clear,
there is time to make up your mind.
Challenge yourself, enjoy the adventure,
and leave indecision behind.

You choose the direction in which you walk,
   you speak the words you wish to talk.
No one can tell you just what you should do,
   your journey is yours, it's all up to you.

It's your choice to enjoy all the good things you've earned;

living is easy, when you use what you've learned.

Smile

A smile is one of life's most neglected gifts, and the one most easily shared. Whether it's shared in the same room or sent around the world in the wind, a smile can brighten the darkest of days. We all know how wonderful it is to be on the receiving end of a beautiful smile, and yet it is often the last thing we think of sharing with someone else. A smile should be the first thing you see in the mirror in the morning and the last thing you see at night.

A smile shared with a loved one is wrapped in warmth, tenderness, and emotion; a smile shared with a friend is covered with kindness, support, and respect; and a smile shared with a stranger is mixed with hope, strength, and light. It only takes a second to show how much you are interested in someone or how much you appreciate an event, a place, or just the moment. It is a silent agreement, a reflection of fondness.

As newborns, we put smiles on the faces of those who surround us—it is the first thing we learn to do. Even before realizing we have fingers and toes we are able to respond to a smile. I have witnessed in my lifetime the full circle of smiling, as it is also the last thing we are capable of doing before we cross the bridge. It calms those around us by helping them believe we are at peace and looking forward to our next journey. So in between birth and our final moments, we should perfect and pass on as many smiles as we can.

Remember today as you embark on your journey that the simplest things in life are the most appreciated, and the warmest gift you can give, to others and yourself, is the gift of a sincere smile. Call on your fondest memories in your quiet moments and smile to yourself. Think of places you would like to be to get you through a dull moment. Smile at a bird in a tree or a dog that crosses your path and see how wonderful you feel inside. Smile at yourself for accomplishing a task or for simply just being you, and see how wonderful you look on the outside.

Know that the smile you share today will come back to you tenfold tomorrow.

How wonderful it is just to greet a new day,
to smile back at the sun as it starts its sashay.
Once we've stepped from the blanket of night,
we can share from our souls the brightest of light.

You can cause a small ripple that flows through the day,
from person to person when you give smiles away.
They are free for the taking and worth more than money,
and your smile can make any cloudy day sunny.

Remember this rule to help keep you on track:
when you send out a smile, a smile comes back.

The smile you share as you get on with your day
helps to move obstacles that get in your way.

It's always enjoyable when you giggle inside,
but it's much more rewarding to smile really wide.

Have fun with your life and choose to smile,
>	with every ounce of your being;
>	laugh from your belly until it hurts,
>	let others enjoy what you're seeing.

Change will be and then you will see
what positive thinking can do:
you will find, that in any bind,
a smile will get you through.

Life is so much easier when you live it with a smile,
and you'll notice that the side effects will last for quite a while.
So focus all your energy on what's positive and real,
enjoy the way the world looks, and how it makes you feel.

Laugher should often be prescribed,
for fixing up your ills,
when used along with smiles each day,
it's cheaper than the pills.

Put on a smile when you get dressed this morning,
it goes with all you wear;
it matches everything you own,
and it's something you can share.

Live in awe of the beauty you see,
and be happy in knowing that smiling is free.

Opportunity

When opportunity knocks, will you hear it? And when you hear the knock, will you recognize the opportunity? Sometimes waiting for that knock on the door is just not enough. In fact, by waiting you may be missing out—every now and then you have to get creative. You may need to fabricate your own doors and make sure they open for you.

Have you ever thought of trying out the same old things with new ambition? Or have you become uncomfortable with change? If you do not look for openings, then you will fail to see chances for growth, so take the opportunity to change the way you look at things. Whatever you find yourself doing right now, today, could very well be your moment to excel at something. Why not? Can you take step back and look at what you are doing from a different perspective? Can you tweak or improve on what you are doing just a little to facilitate new opportunities? Is there an opportunity for change in your life right at this very moment?

When you wake each morning and open your eyes, remember that it is a brand new day full of brand new opportunities. Yesterday is a memory and tomorrow will get here in time, so take this chance to do something new today, for you. Change the way you do things, have some fun, brush your teeth with your left hand, take a different route to work, wear a smile all day, be happy being you. Notice your surroundings, notice your co-workers. If they are not smiling, then share a smile with them. If you are outside, then breathe, feel the sun on your face, live, and make your life worthwhile.

Life is indeed full of opportunities. If we choose to recognize them for what they are, we become more in tune with them and learn how to create them for ourselves. We become the carpenters of our future by using the tools at our disposal to construct our own opportunities.

Believe in yourself, don't wait for a knock—open the door and welcome change.

Before an echo can reverberate
you have to shout hello,
and in order to actually get anywhere
you have to get up and go.

The world will pass you by, my friend, if all you're doing is waiting,
you need to dance to those drums you hear—it's really quite elating.

Don't wait for that day to finally arrive,
it's already been a while;
today is the day to make a minute
to show the world your style.

We can't enjoy flying till we spread out our wings,
    so feel the wind, and the joy that it brings.
We can't enjoy flying till we spread out our wings,
    to soar to great heights and love what life brings.

Walk your path with your head held high,
keep the horizon clear in sight,
opportunity knocks but only once,
and you'll need to know it's right.

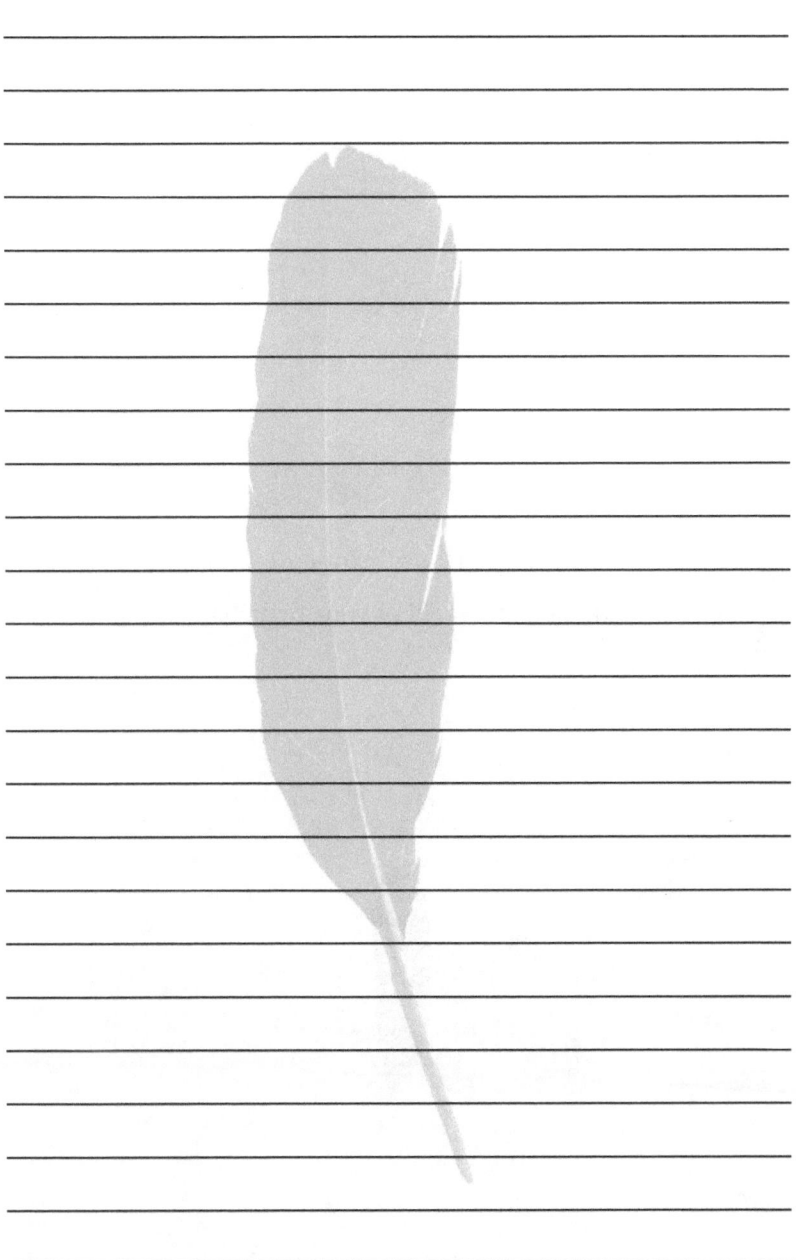

Grasp the ring of happenstance,
and enjoy the thrill of your first chance.

To say it's possible to live your dreams
is an understatement at best,
but you need to climb the tallest mountain
to get a clear view of the rest.

Welcome opportunities with an open mind,
and believe in what you can do,
the end result of giving your all
is always what's best for you.

Things happen for a reason, at least that's what we're told,
so go ahead and cross that bridge before you grow too old.

Mornings happen, are you used to them yet?
Are you happy to greet the day?
Does your energy lead as you get out of bed,
or does your pillow make you stay?
Today is a day you haven't lived yet,
do you wonder what you might see?
Rest assured that with no effort at all,
you will have the chance to just BE.

Being You

What does "being you" mean to you? And are you aware of the times when you are not being you? Do you wake in the morning and feel like yourself and then go to the mirror and see someone totally different? Do you have the self-confidence and the strength to be yourself in a crowd, or on a stage, or are you a quiet, more reserved individual who finds a voice through other means? Either way, you are the only one who can determine how comfortable you are with yourself.

It can take a lifetime to grow comfortable with who you are, and you may often be called upon to be stronger than you think you are or more logical than you want to be. In uncomfortable and awkward situations, simply believing in yourself will help get you through. And there are times when just sharing a smile with those around you will help others believe in you and trust in who you are.

If you are where you want to be in life, and if you are comfortable with who you are, then the energy you put out to the world will be reflected back to you by people just like you—people who are proud and who like being themselves. Find the energy that flows within you and directs you to places where being you is easy and accepted. Being you means being real, and believing in yourself can often make all the difference in terms of your happiness.

Choosing to be yourself is always the right choice. Your friends liked who you were when they met you, and as long as you don't change into something you're not, they will continue to be your friends, because you are you. Stay true to yourself, be proud of yourself, do the things that make you happy, and share in the things that others do to make them happy. You are you for the rest of your life. Being you shouldn't be a full-time job: it should be your most relaxing hobby.

Have fun. Be real. Believe in you.

You can't help another until you help yourself—
you're the only one who can.
As you look in the mirror you need to confirm
that you are your biggest fan.

You know very well that what I say is true:
your eyes have the means to see beauty in you.
See yourself through the eyes of another,
the beauty of you that you need to uncover.

Your beauty is yours and it's more than skin deep—
it's not what you can see;
it's all about the you inside,
the you who loves to BE.

We need pride from within to guide us without,
and a voice from our soul to diminish the doubt.

Some will try to break you down,
because they think you're weak,
but the strength you hide that is your essence
is found where they can't seek.

Believe in you with strength and pride,
hold on to your stalwart convictions;
enjoy the moments as you write your story,
then share your grand depiction.

Be real today because you can, don't hide behind a shroud;
step out from the crowd you're in: stand up and be proud.

Draw each breath and love life being you,
let nothing get in your way.
Enjoy who you are and all that you do
while being yourself today.

Gaze upon an evening star, and marvel in its light.
Believe in who you really are and let your soul take flight.

Never give up on being yourself—there's a reason that you are unique: you're the only one who can open the door to the happiness you seek.

Give yourself some appropriate credit, whenever it is due, because you really are the best at simply being you.

So with all I've said, and all you've read,
do you have a better view?
Have you sat for a moment and reflected on life,
and do you love just being you?
Trust in yourself and the choices you make,
share your smile while you're living.
You are one of a kind and should be proud
of the energy that you're giving.
I bet you didn't think there would be a test,
but I write these words to share,
the importance of always believing in you,
and loving life out there.

Acknowledgments

I would like to thank the people in my life who have been there to help me along this new and uncharted path on which I walk.

Rachel Small - Editor, Faultless Finish Editing
Carrie Mumford - Proofreader
Jessee Wise - Illustrator
Fiona Raven - Designer

And to the souls in my life who have given me strength, support and inspiration, this adventure would not have happened without you all. Special thanks to all those who share my path, my life and my smiles.

About the Author

Robert (BawB) Chomany is the author of the BawB's Raven Feathers series, pure and simple inspirational books. He was born in Calgary, Alberta, with a clear view of the mountains to the west. These mountains eventually drew Bob in, and he spent many years living in the company of nature, exploring his spiritual side.

Bob pursues his many interests with passion. You are just as likely to find him twisting a wrench, or riding his motorcycle, as you are to find him holding a pen, writing.

Bob still lives in Calgary, where he finds happiness by simply living with a smile and sharing his words of wisdom with others.

www.ingramcontent.com/pod-product-compliance
Lightning Source LLC
Chambersburg PA
CBHW032046290426
44110CB00012B/974